# IMAGINE ME

### Ella Louise Dawson     Larry Dawson

## FOR EVERY CHILD WHO HAS AN IMAGINATION

WORKBOOK PRESS LLC
187 E Warm Springs Rd,
Suite B285, Las Vegas, NV 89119, USA

Website:    https://workbookpress.com/
Hotline:    1-888-818-4856
Email:      admin@workbookpress.com

Ordering Information:
Quantity sales. Special discounts are available on quantity purchases by corporations, associations, and others.
For details, contact the publisher at the address above.

ISBN-13:        978-1-957618-80-7 (Paperback Version)
                978-1-957618-81-4 (Digital Version)

REV. DATE:    02/28/2022

# IMAGINE ME

By Larry and Louise Dawson

# DEDICATION

In Memory of My Sister :
Anna Marie Williams. AKA Marie
November - 04- 1953 - 2000


Marie had a beautiful personality.
Marie would make you laugh even when you were having your worse day.
Marie could bring the Sunshine through a cloudy day.
Marie loved stuffed animals and baby dolls.
Marie's favorite song was Silent Night.
Our Loving Anna Marie
MUCH LOVE ALWAYS.


In Memory of Our Xavior:
Xavior Xa'on Beck
April-17-2012-April-2014


Xavior captivating and loving smile, and his gentle touch.
Xavior captivating eyes, how they had the magic touch.
Xavior, You'll Always Be With Us.


In Memory of Our Grandparents;
Earnest Dawson
Lucille Dawson
What we loved most about them is Earnest and Lucille were there for us no

matter what.
Love You Always, Forever In Our Hearts.


In Memory of Our Grandmother:
Julia Mae Cochrane-Jones
You Are Truly Missed


To our dad:
Lee Roy Cochrane Sr.
June 30, 1937 - February 10, 2021
Thank you for being a part all of our lives.
You Are Truly Missed!


Iteia LaDawn Colyar
July 5, 1980-February 26, 2022
To Teia (My Cuddder).
You will always be forever missed,
from our phone calls from sunup to sun down,
or just being there for each other when things got rough.
I love and miss you!

# ACKNOWLEDGEMENT

Our deepest appreciation to:
ELLIS DAWSON, JALAYAH AND JAMAR JONES for drawing some of the pictures that will appear in our book. We want to thank all of our Family for the support and time that they gave us as we walked down this journey together Much Love.

AUTHOR: MR. LEWIS COLYAR
For believing in Ms. Louise Dawson and Mr. Larry Dawson, and for helping us bring our dream to a reality.

MISS KEIRRA DAVIS
A very Talented and Brilliant young lady who brought our cover story to life before our eyes, even before it was sent into our Illustration team at the publisher.

HEATHER YOUNG, KAREN GRANT AND THE ILLUSTRATION TEAM, Beautiful Job!!!

# INTRODUCTION

## IMAGINE ME

This book is to inspire all children of the world to use their imagination. To experience how to explore the world thought their eyes and mine. It is fun to see how it would be to run a race out in space ,to fly on a magical kite in the sky while the beautiful birds are flying by. HI I am Ella Dawson the writer ,Hi I am Larry Dawson jr. the co-writer. We wrote this book because over the years we have had the pleasure of enjoying our little people in our family growing up using their imagination as they played. It is a beautiful thing to see and yes sometimes to be a part of it. We hope that your family will enjoy reading this book together and Yes !!!

## IMAGINE IS GREAT!

Mr. Larry and I have provided you with extra paper so that you can use your imagination. ENJOY!!.We were so excited when we wrote this book in 2008.We think that it so Awesome and we will always be thankful to God whom has blessed us to share it with all the children of the world.

Imagine me drawing a Blue, Green and Yellow rainbow tree.

Can you see how pretty that will be?

Imagine me in outer space with a Martian running a race

Who do you think will be in first place!!

ARW!

Imagine me in a Pirate Ship out in the open seas looking for gold, that's where you will find me and my crew.

With a Treasure map in my hand, me and my crew has just found land.

Imagine me riding down the icy slopes with a whale as my friend.

As the whale flap his fin the icy water splash and I yelled, "I'm going in"

Imagine me as a knight with a pet dragon.

After a long days' fight, my dragon and I went to grab a bite.

Imagine me as a Cheetah running through the wild with speed of lighting it makes me so proud.

My Legs are strong. My eyes are sharp. I see better in the dark!

"Hi, I am Kaydon Johnson. Look at what my imagination can do!"

I am an artist YOU CAN BE ONE TOO!!!!!!!!!!